About The Holy Bible
A Lecture

by

Robert G. Ingersoll

**ABOUT THE HOLY BIBLE
A Lecture**
by Robert G. Ingersoll

Copyright © 2023

All Rights reserved.

ISBN: 978-93-59950-98-3

Published by

DOUBLE 9 BOOKS

2/13-B, Ansari Road
Daryaganj, New Delhi – 110002
info@double9books.com
www.double9books.com
Tel. 011-40042856

ABOUT THE AUTHOR

Robert Green Ingersoll (August 11, 1833 – July 21, 1899) was an American lawyer, writer, and orator who campaigned in support of agnosticism during the Golden Age of Free Thought. Robert Ingersoll was born in the town of Dresden, New York. His father, John Ingersoll, was an abolitionist-friendly Congregationalist pastor whose radical views prompted him and his family to move frequently. While American revivalist Charles G. Finney was on tour in Europe, Rev. John Ingersoll filled in as preacher for a while. Rev. Ingersoll continued as co-pastor/associate pastor with Finney for a few months after his return. However, as The Elmira Telegram reported in 1890, the elder Ingersoll's subsequent pastoral experiences had a bad impact on young Robert. Colonel Ingersoll was born and raised in a devoutly Christian family, despite being the most well-known of American unbelievers for many years. His father, John Ingersoll, was a Congregationalist preacher and a man of note in his day, a keen thinker, a logical and eloquent speaker, broad-minded and generously accepting of other people's points of view. The prevalent perception that attributes Ingersoll's infidelity mostly to his father's strict orthodoxy and the austere and dreary conditions in which he grew up is completely incorrect.

CONTENTS

THERE are many millions of people who believe the Bible to be the inspired word of God—millions who think that this book is staff and guide, counselor and consoler; that it fills the present with peace and the future with hope—millions who believe that it is the fountain of law, justice and mercy, and that to its wise and benign teachings the world is indebted for its liberty, wealth and civilization—millions who imagine that this book is a revelation from the wisdom and love of God to the brain and heart of man—millions who regard this book as a torch that conquers the darkness of death, and pours its radiance on another world—a world without a tear. They forget its ignorance and savagery, its hatred of liberty, its religious persecution; they remember heaven, but they forget the dungeon of eternal pain.

I
THE ORIGIN OF THE BIBLE

A FEW wandering families—poor, wretched; without education, art or power; descendants of those who had been enslaved for four hundred years; ignorant as the inhabitants of Central Africa—had just escaped from their masters to the desert of Sinai.

Their leader was Moses, a man who had been raised in the family of Pharaoh, and had been taught the law and mythology of Egypt. For the purpose of controlling his followers he pretended that he was instructed and assisted by Jehovah, the god of these wanderers.

Everything that happened was attributed to the interference of this god. Moses declared that he met this god face to face; that on Sinai's top from the hands of this god he had received the tables of stone on which, by the finger of this god, the Ten Commandments had been written, and that, in addition to this, Jehovah had made known the sacrifices and ceremonies that were pleasing to him and the laws by which the people should be governed.

In this way the Jewish religion and the Mosaic Code were established.

It is now claimed that this religion and these laws were and are revealed and established for all mankind.

At that time these wanderers had no commerce with other nations—they had no written language—they could neither read nor write. They had no means by which they could make this revelation known to other nations, and so it remained buried in the jargon of a few ignorant, impoverished and unknown tribes for more than two thousand years.

Many centuries after Moses, the leader, was dead—many centuries after all his followers had passed away—the Pentateuch was written, the work of many writers, and to give it force and authority it was claimed that Moses was the author.

We now know that the Pentateuch was not written by Moses.

Towns are mentioned that were not in existence when Moses lived.

Money, not coined until centuries after his death, is mentioned.

So, many of the laws were not applicable to wanderers on the desert—laws about agriculture, about the sacrifice of oxen, sheep and doves, about the weaving of cloth, about ornaments of gold and silver, about the cultivation of land, about harvest, about the threshing of grain, about houses and temples, about cities of refuge, and about many other subjects of no possible application to a few starving wanderers over the sands and rocks.

It is now not only admitted by intelligent and honest theologians that Moses was not the author of the Pentateuch, but they all admit that no one knows who the authors were, or who wrote any one of these books, or a chapter or a line. We know that the books were not written in the same generation; that they were not all written by one person; that they are filled with mistakes and contradictions.

It is also admitted that Joshua did not write the book that bears his name, because it refers to events that did not happen until long after his death.

No one knows, or pretends to know, the author of Judges; all we know is that it was written centuries after all the judges had ceased to exist. No one knows the author of Ruth, nor of First and Second Samuel; all we know is that Samuel did not write the books that bear his name. In the 25th chapter of First Samuel is an account of Samuel's death, and in the 27th chapter is an account of the raising of Samuel by the Witch of Endor.

No one knows the author of First and Second Kings or First and Second Chronicles; all we know is that these books are of no value.

We know that the Psalms were not written by David. In the Psalms the Captivity is spoken of, and that did not happen until about five hundred years after David slept with his fathers.

We know that Solomon did not write the Proverbs or the Song; that Isaiah was not the author of the book that bears his name; that no one knows the author of Job, Ecclesiastes or Esther, or of any book in the Old Testament, with the exception of Ezra.

We know that God is not mentioned or in any way referred to in the book of Esther. We know, too, that the book is cruel, absurd and impossible.

God is not mentioned in the Song of Solomon, the best book in the Old Testament.

And we know that Ecclesiastes was written by an unbeliever.

We know, too, that the Jews themselves had not decided as to what books were inspired—were authentic—until the second century after Christ.

We know that the idea of inspiration was of slow growth, and that the inspiration was determined by those who had certain ends to accomplish.

II
IS THE OLD TESTAMENT INSPIRED?

If it is, it should be a book that no man—no number of men—could produce.

It should contain the perfection of philosophy.

It should perfectly accord with every fact in nature.

There should be no mistakes in astronomy, geology, or as to any subject or science.

Its morality should be the highest, the purest.

Its laws and regulations for the control of conduct should be just, wise, perfect, and perfectly adapted to the accomplishment of the ends desired.

It should contain nothing calculated to make man cruel, revengeful, vindictive or infamous.

It should be filled with intelligence, justice, purity, honesty, mercy and the spirit of liberty.

It should be opposed to strife and war, to slavery and lust, to ignorance, credulity and superstition.

It should develop the brain and civilize the heart.

It should satisfy the heart and brain of the best and wisest.

It should be true.

Does the Old Testament satisfy this standard?

Is there anything in the Old Testament—in history, in theory, in law, in government, in morality, in science—above and beyond the ideas, the beliefs, the customs and prejudices of its authors and the people among whom they lived?

Is there one ray of light from any supernatural source?

The ancient Hebrews believed that this earth was the centre of the universe, and that the sun, moon and stars were specks in the sky.

With this the Bible agrees.

They thought the earth was flat, with four corners; that the sky, the firmament, was solid—the floor of Jehovah's house.

The Bible teaches the same.

They imagined that the sun journeyed about the earth, and that by stopping the sun the day could be lengthened.

The Bible agrees with this.

They believed that Adam and Eve were the first man and woman; that they had been created but a few years before, and that they, the Hebrews, were their direct descendants.

This the Bible teaches.

If anything is, or can be, certain, the writers of the Bible were mistaken about creation, astronomy, geology; about the causes of phenomena, the origin of evil and the cause of death.

Now, it must be admitted that if an Infinite Being is the author of the Bible, he knew all sciences, all facts, and could not have made a mistake.

If, then, there are mistakes, misconceptions, false theories, ignorant myths and blunders in the Bible, it must have been written by finite beings; that is to say, by ignorant and mistaken men.

Nothing can be clearer than this.

For centuries the Church insisted that the Bible was absolutely true; that it contained no mistakes; that the story of creation was true; that its astronomy and geology were in accord with the facts; that the scientists who differed with the Old Testament were infidels and atheists.

Now this has changed. The educated Christians admit that the writers of the Bible were not inspired as to any science. They now say that God, or Jehovah, did not inspire the writers of his book for the purpose of instructing the world about astronomy, geology or any science. They now admit that the inspired men who wrote the Old Testament knew nothing about any science, and that they wrote about the earth and stars, the sun and moon, in accordance with the general ignorance of the time.

It required many centuries to force the theologians to this admission. Reluctantly, full of malice and hatred, the priests retired from the field, leaving the victory with science.

They took another position:

They declared that the authors, or rather the writers, of the Bible were inspired in spiritual and moral things; that Jehovah wanted to make known to his children his will and his infinite love for his children; that Jehovah, seeing his people wicked, ignorant and depraved, wished to make them merciful and just, wise and spiritual, and that the Bible is inspired in its laws, in the religion it teaches and in its ideas of government.

This is the issue now. Is the Bible any nearer right in its ideas of justice, of mercy, of morality or of religion than in its conception of the sciences?

Is it moral?

It upholds slavery—it sanctions polygamy.

Could a devil have done worse?

Is it merciful?

In war it raised the black flag; it commanded the destruction, the massacre, of all—of the old, infirm, and helpless—of wives and babes.

Were its laws inspired?

Hundreds of offenses were punished with death. To pick up sticks on Sunday, to murder your father on Monday, were equal crimes. There is in the literature of the world no bloodier code. The law of revenge—of retaliation—was the law of Jehovah. An eye for an eye, a tooth for a tooth, a limb for a limb.

This is savagery—not philosophy.

Is it just and reasonable?

The Bible is opposed to religious toleration—to religious liberty. Whoever differed with the majority was stoned to death. Investigation was a crime. Husbands were ordered to denounce and to assist in killing their unbelieving wives.

It is the enemy of Art. "Thou shalt make no graven image." This was the death of Art.

Palestine never produced a painter or a sculptor.

Is the Bible civilized?

It upholds lying, larceny, robbery, murder, the selling of diseased meat to strangers, and even the sacrifice of human beings to Jehovah.

Is it philosophical?

It teaches that the sins of a people can be transferred to an animal—to a goat. It makes maternity an offense, for which a sin offering had to be made.

It was wicked to give birth to a boy, and twice as wicked to give birth to a girl.

To make hair-oil like that used by the priests was an offense punishable with death.

The blood of a bird killed over running water was regarded as medicine.

Would a civilized God daub his altars with the blood of oxen, lambs and doves? Would he make all his priests butchers? Would he delight in the smell of burning flesh?

III
THE TEN COMMANDMENTS

SOME Christian lawyers—some eminent and stupid judges—have said and still say, that the Ten Commandments are the foundation of all law.

Nothing could be more absurd. Long before these Commandments were given there were codes of laws in India and Egypt—laws against murder, perjury, larceny, adultery and fraud. Such laws are as old as human society; as old as the love of life; as old as industry; as the idea of prosperity; as old as human love.

All of the Ten Commandments that are good were old; all that were new are foolish. If Jehovah had been civilized he would have left out the commandment about keeping the Sabbath, and in its place would have said: "Thou shalt not enslave thy fellow-men." He would have omitted the one about swearing, and said: "The man shall have but one wife, and the woman but one husband." He would have left out the one about graven images, and in its stead would have said: "Thou shalt not wage wars of extermination, and thou shalt not unsheathe the sword except in self-defense."

If Jehovah had been civilized, how much grander the Ten Commandments would have been.

All that we call progress—the enfranchisement of man, of labor, the substitution of imprisonment for death, of fine for imprisonment, the destruction of polygamy, the establishing of free speech, of the rights of conscience; in short, all that has tended to the development and civilization of man; all the results of investigation, observation, experience and free thought; all that man has accomplished for the benefit of man since the close of the Dark Ages—has been done in spite of the Old Testament.

Let me further illustrate the morality, the mercy, the philosophy and goodness of the Old Testament:

THE STORY OF ACHAN.

Joshua took the City of Jericho. Before the fall of the city he declared that all the spoil taken should be given to the Lord.

In spite of this order Achan secreted a garment, some silver and gold.

Afterwards Joshua tried to take the city of Ai. He failed and many of his soldiers were slain.

Joshua sought for the cause of his defeat and he found that Achan had secreted a garment, two hundred shekels of silver and a wedge of gold. To this Achan confessed.

And thereupon Joshua took Achan, his sons and his daughters, his oxen and his sheep—stoned them all to death and burned their bodies.

There is nothing to show that the sons and daughters had committed any crime. Certainly, the oxen and sheep should not have been stoned to death for the crime of their owner. This was the justice, the mercy, of Jehovah!

After Joshua had committed this crime, with the help of Jehovah he captured the city of Ai.

THE STORY OF ELISHA.

"And he went up thence unto Bethel, and as he was going up by the way there came forth little children out of the city and mocked him, and said unto him, 'Go up, thou baldhead.

"And he turned back and looked at them, and cursed them in the name of the Lord. And there came forth two she-bears out of the wood and tore forty and two children of them."

This was the work of the good God—the merciful Jehovah!

THE STORY OF DANIEL.

King Darius had honored and exalted Daniel, and the native princes were jealous. So they induced the King to sign a decree to the effect that any man who should make a petition to any god or man except to King Darius, for thirty days, should be cast into the den of lions.

Afterwards these men found that Daniel, with his face toward Jerusalem, prayed three times a day to Jehovah.

Thereupon Daniel was cast into the den of lions; a stone was placed at the mouth of the den and sealed with the King's seal.

The King passed a bad night. The next morning he went to the den and cried out to Daniel. Daniel answered and told the King that God had sent his angel and shut the mouths of the lions.

Daniel was taken out alive and well, and the King was converted and believed in Daniel's god.

Darius, being then a believer in the true God, sent for the men who had accused Daniel, and for their wives and their children, and cast them all into the lions' den.

"And the lions had the mastery of them, and brake all their bones in pieces, or ever they came at the bottom of the pit."

What had the wives and little children done? How had they offended King Darius, the believer in Jehovah? Who protected Daniel? Jehovah! Who failed to protect the innocent wives and children? Jehovah!

THE STORY OF JOSEPH.

Pharaoh had a dream, and this dream was interpreted by Joseph.

According to this interpretation there was to be in Egypt seven years of plenty, followed by seven years of famine. Joseph advised Pharaoh to buy all the surplus of the seven plentiful years and store it up against the years of famine.

Pharaoh appointed Joseph as his minister or agent, and ordered him to buy the grain of the plentiful years.

Then came the famine. The people came to the King for help. He told them to go to Joseph and do as he said.

Joseph sold corn to the Egyptians until all their money was gone—until he had it all.

When the money was gone the people said: "Give us corn and we will give you our cattle."

Joseph let them have corn until all their cattle, their horses and their flocks had been given to him.

Then the people said: "Give us corn and we will give you our lands."

So Joseph let them have corn until all their lands were gone.

But the famine continued, and so the poor wretches sold themselves, and they became the servants of Pharoah.

Then Joseph gave them seed, and made an agreement with them that they should forever give one-fifth of all they raised to Pharaoh.

Who enabled Joseph to interpret the dream of Pharaoh? Jehovah! Did he know at the time that Joseph would use the information thus given to rob and enslave the people of Egypt? Yes. Who produced the famine? Jehovah!

It is perfectly apparent that the Jews did not think of Jehovah as the God of Egypt—the God of all the world. He was their God, and theirs alone. Other nations had gods, but Jehovah was the greatest of all. He hated other nations and other gods, and abhorred all religions except the worship of himself.

IV
WHAT IS IT ALL WORTH?

WILL some Christian scholar tell us the value of Genesis?

We know that it is not true—that it contradicts itself. There are two accounts of the creation in the first and second chapters. In the first account birds and beasts were created before man.

In the second, man was created before the birds and beasts.

In the first, fowls are made out of the water.

In the second, fowls are made out of the ground.

In the first, Adam and Eve are created together.

In the second, Adam is made; then the beasts and birds, and then Eve is created from one of Adam's ribs.

These stories are far older than the Pentateuch.

Persian: God created the world in six days, a man called Adama, a woman called Evah, and then rested.

The Etruscan, Babylonian, Phoenician, Chaldean and the Egyptian stories are much the same.

The Persians, Greeks, Egyptians, Chinese and Hindus have their Garden of Eden and the Tree of Life.

So the Persians, the Babylonians, the Nubians, the people of Southern India, all had the story of the Fall of Man and the subtle serpent.

The Chinese say that sin came into the world by the disobedience of woman. And even the Tahitians tell us that man was created from the earth, and the first woman from one of his bones.

All these stories are equally authentic and of equal value to the world, and all the authors were equally inspired.

We know also that the story of the Flood is much older than the book of Genesis, and we know besides that it is not true.

We know that this story in Genesis was copied from the Chaldean. There you find all about the rain, the ark, the animals, the dove that was sent out three times, and the mountain on which the ark rested.

So the Hindus, Chinese, Parsees, Persians, Greeks, Mexicans and Scandinavians have substantially the same story.

We also knew that the account of the Tower of Babel is an ignorant and childish fable.

What then is left in this inspired book of Genesis? Is there a word calculated to develop the heart or brain? Is there an elevated thought—any great principle—anything poetic—any word that bursts into blossom?

Is there anything except a dreary and detailed statement of things that never happened?

Is there anything in Exodus calculated to make men generous, loving and noble?

Is it well to teach children that God tortured the innocent cattle of the Egyptians—bruised them to death with hailstones—on account of the sins of Pharoah?

Does it make us merciful to believe that God killed the firstborn of the Egyptians—the firstborn of the poor and suffering people—of the poor girl working at the mill—because of the wickedness of the King?

Can we believe that the gods of Egypt worked miracles? Did they change water into blood, and sticks into serpents?

In Exodus there is not one original thought or line of value.

We know, if we know anything, that this book was written by savages—savages who believed in slavery, polygamy and wars of extermination. We know that the story told is impossible, and that the miracles were never performed. This book admits that there are other gods besides Jehovah. In the 17th chapter is this verse: "Now I know that the Lord is greater than all gods, for, in the thing wherein they dealt proudly, he was above them."

So, in this blessed book is taught the duty of human sacrifice—the sacrifice of babes.

In the 22d chapter is this command: "Thou shalt not delay to offer the first of thy ripe fruits and of thy liquors: the first born of thy sons thou shalt give unto me."

Has Exodus been a help or a hindrance to the human race?

Take from Exodus the laws common to all nations, and is there anything of value left?

Is there anything in Leviticus of importance? Is there a chapter worth reading? What interest have we in the clothes of priests, the curtains and candles of the tabernacle, the tongs and shovels of the altar or the hair-oil used by the Levites?

Of what use the cruel code, the frightful punishments, the curses, the falsehoods and the miracles of this ignorant and infamous book?

And what is there in the book of Numbers—with its sacrifices and water of jealousy, with its shew-bread and spoons, its kids and fine flour, its oil and candlesticks, its cucumbers, onions and manna—to assist and instruct mankind? What interest have we in the rebellion of Korah, the water of separation, the ashes of a red heifer, the brazen serpent, the water that followed the people uphill and down for forty years, and the inspired donkey of the prophet Balaam? Have these absurdities and cruelties—these childish, savage superstitions—helped to civilize the world?

Is there anything in Joshua—with its wars, its murders and massacres, its swords dripping with the blood of mothers and babes, its tortures, maimings and mutilations, its fraud and fury, its hatred and revenge—calculated to improve the world?

Does not every chapter shock the heart of a good man? Is it a book to be read by children?

The book of Joshua is as merciless as famine, as ferocious as the heart of a wild beast. It is a history—a justification—a sanctification of nearly every crime.

The book of Judges is about the same, nothing but war and bloodshed; the horrible story of Jael and Sisera; of Gideon and his trumpets and pitchers; of Jephtha and his daughter, whom he murdered to please Jehovah.

Here we find the story of Samson, in which a sun-god is changed to a Hebrew giant.

Read this book of Joshua—read of the slaughter of women, of wives, of mothers and babes—read its impossible miracles, its ruthless crimes, and all done according to the commands of Jehovah, and tell me whether this book is calculated to make us forgiving, generous and loving.

I admit that the history of Ruth is in some respects a beautiful and touching story; that it is naturally told, and that her love for Naomi was deep and pure. But in the matter of courtship we would hardly advise our daughters to follow the example of Ruth. Still, we must remember that Ruth was a widow.

Is there anything worth reading in the first and second books of Samuel? Ought a prophet of God to hew a captured king in pieces? Is the story of the ark, its capture and return of importance to us? Is it possible that it was right, just and merciful to kill fifty thousand men because they had looked into a box? Of what use to us are the wars of Saul and David, the stories of Goliath and the Witch of Endor? Why should Jehovah have killed Uzzah for putting forth his hand to steady the ark, and forgiven David for murdering Uriah and stealing his wife?

According to "Samuel," David took a census of the people. This excited the wrath of Jehovah, and as a punishment he allowed David to choose seven years of famine, a flight of three months from pursuing enemies, or three days of pestilence. David, having confidence in God, chose the three days of pestilence; and, thereupon, God, the compassionate, on account of the sin of David, killed seventy thousand innocent men!

Under the same circumstances, what would a devil have done?

Is there anything in First and Second Kings that suggests the idea of inspiration?

When David is dying he tells his son Solomon to murder Joab—not to let his hoar head go down to the grave in peace. With his last breath he commands his son to bring down the hoar head of Shimei to the grave with blood. Having uttered these merciful words, the good David, the man after God's heart, slept with his fathers.

Was it necessary to inspire the man who wrote the history of the building of the temple, the story of the visit of the Queen of Sheba, or to tell the number of Solomon's wives?

What care we for the withering of Jereboam's hand, the prophecy of Jehu, or the story of Elijah and the ravens?

Can we believe that Elijah brought flames from heaven, or that he went at last to Paradise in a chariot of fire?

Can we believe in the multiplication of the widow's oil by Elisha, that an army was smitten with blindness, or that an axe floated in the water?

Does it civilize us to read about the beheading of the seventy sons of Ahab, the putting out of the eyes of Zedekiah and the murder of his sons? Is there one word in First and Second Kings calculated to make men better?

First and Second Chronicles is but a re-telling of what is told in First and Second Kings. The same old stories—a little left out, a little added, but in no respect made better or worse.

The book of Ezra is of no importance. He tells us that Cyrus, King of Persia, issued a proclamation for building a temple at Jerusalem, and that he declared Jehovah to be the real and only God.

Nothing could be more absurd. Ezra tells us about the return from captivity, the building of the temple, the dedication, a few prayers, and this is all. This book is of no importance, of no use.

Nehemiah is about the same, only it tells of the building of the wall, the complaints of the people about taxes, a list of those who returned from Babylon, a catalogue of those who dwelt at Jerusalem, and the dedication of the walls.

Not a word in Nehemiah worth reading.

Then comes the book of Esther:

In this we are told that King Ahasueras was intoxicated; that he sent for his Queen, Vashti, to come and show herself to him and his guests. Vashti refused to appear.

This maddened the King, and he ordered that from every province the most beautiful girls should be brought before him that he might choose one in place of Vashti.

Among others was brought Esther, a Jewess. She was chosen and became the wife of the King. Then a gentleman by the name of Haman wanted to have all the Jews killed, and the King, not knowing that Esther was of that race, signed a decree that all the Jews should be killed.

Through the efforts of Mordecai and Esther the decree was annulled and the Jews were saved.

Haman prepared a gallows on which to have Mordecai hanged, but the good Esther so managed matters that Haman and his ten sons were hanged on the gallows that Haman had built, and the Jews were allowed to murder more than seventy-five thousand of the King's subjects.

This is the inspired story of Esther.

In the book of Job we find some elevated sentiments, some sublime and foolish thoughts, something of the wonder and sublimity of nature, the joys and sorrows of life; but the story is infamous.

Some of the Psalms are good, many are indifferent, and a few are infamous. In them are mingled the vices and virtues. There are verses that elevate; verses that degrade. There are prayers for forgiveness and revenge. In the literature of the world there is nothing more heartless, more infamous, than the 109th Psalm.

In the Proverbs there is much shrewdness, many pithy and prudent maxims, many wise sayings. The same ideas are expressed in many ways—the wisdom of economy and silence, the dangers of vanity and idleness. Some are trivial, some are foolish, and many are wise. These proverbs are not generous—not altruistic. Sayings to the same effect are found among all nations.

Ecclesiastes is the most thoughtful book in the Bible. It was written by an unbeliever—a philosopher—an agnostic. Take out the interpolations, and it is in accordance with the thought of the Nineteenth Century. In this book are found the most philosophic and poetic passages in the Bible.

After crossing the desert of death and crime—after reading the Pentateuch, Joshua, Judges, Samuel, Kings and Chronicles—it is delightful to reach this grove of palms, called the "Song of Solomon." A drama of love—of human love; a poem without Jehovah—a poem born of the heart and true to the divine instincts of the soul.

"I sleep, but my heart waketh."

Isaiah is the work of several. Its swollen words, its vague imagery, its prophecies and curses, its ravings against kings and nations, its laughter at the wisdom of man, its hatred of joy, have not the slightest tendency to increase the well-being of man.

In this book is recorded the absurdest of all miracles. The shadow on the dial is turned back ten degrees, in order to satisfy Hezekiah that Jehovah will add fifteen years to his life.

In this miracle the world, turning from west to east at the rate of more than a thousand miles an hour, is not only stopped, but made to turn the other way until the shadow on the dial went back ten degrees! Is there in the whole world an intelligent man or woman who believes this impossible falsehood?

Jeremiah contains nothing of importance—no facts of value; nothing but faultfinding, lamentations, croakings, wailings, curses and promises; nothing but famine and prayer, the prosperity of the wicked, the ruin of the Jews, the captivity and return, and at last Jeremiah, the traitor, in the stocks and in prison.

And Lamentations is simply a continuance of the ravings of the same insane pessimist; nothing but dust and sackcloth and ashes, tears and howls, railings and revilings.

And Ezekiel—eating manuscripts, prophesying siege and desolation, with visions of coals of fire, and cherubim, and wheels with eyes, and the type and figure of the boiling pot, and the resurrection of dry bones—is of no use, of no possible value.

With Voltaire, I say that any one who admires Ezekiel should be compelled to dine with him.

Daniel is a disordered dream—a nightmare.

What can be made of this book with its image with a golden head, with breast and arms of silver, with belly and thighs of brass, with legs of iron, and with feet of iron and clay; with its writing on the wall, its den of lions, and its vision of the ram and goat?

Is there anything to be learned from Hosea and his wife? Is there anything of use in Joel, in Amos, in Obadiah? Can we get any good from Jonah and his gourd? Is it possible that God is the real author of Micah and Nahum, of Habakuk and Zephaniah, of Haggai and Malachi and Zechariah, with his red horses, his four horns, his four carpenters, his flying roll, his mountains of brass and the stone with four eyes?

Is there anything in these "inspired" books that has been of benefit to man?

Have they taught us how to cultivate the earth, to build houses, to weave cloth, to prepare food? Have they taught us to paint pictures, to chisel statues, to build bridges, or ships, or anything of beauty or of use? Did we get our ideas of government, of religious freedom, of the liberty of thought, from the Old Testament? Did we get from any of these books a hint of any science? Is there in the "sacred volume" a word, a line, that has added to the wealth, the intelligence and the happiness of mankind? Is there one of the books of the Old Testament as entertaining as Robinson Crusoe, the Travels of Gulliver, or Peter Wilkins and his Flying Wife? Did the author of Genesis know as much about nature as Humboldt, or Darwin, or Haeckel? Is what is called the Mosaic Code as wise or as merciful as the code of any civilized nation? Were the writers of Kings and Chronicles as great historians, as great writers, as Gibbon and Draper? Is Jeremiah or Habakuk equal to Dickens or Thackeray? Can the authors of Job and the Psalms be compared with Shakespeare? Why should we attribute the best to man and the worst to God?

V
WAS JEHOVAH A GOD OF LOVE?

DID these words come from the heart of love?—"When the Lord thy God shall drive them before thee, thou shalt smite them and utterly destroy them; thou shalt make no covenant with them, or show mercy unto them."

"I will heap mischief upon them. I will send mine arrows upon them; they shall be burned with hunger and devoured with burning heat and with bitter destruction."

"I will send the tooth of beasts upon them, with the poison of serpents of the dust."

"The sword without, and terror within, shall destroy both the young man and the virgin; the suckling also with the man of gray hairs."

"Let his children be fatherless and his wife a widow; let his children be continually vagabonds and beg; let them seek their bread also out of their desolate places; let the extortioner catch all that he hath, and let the stranger spoil his labor; let there be none to extend mercy unto him, neither let there be any to favor his fatherless children."

"And thou shalt eat the fruit of thine own body—the flesh of thy sons and daughters."

"And the heaven that is over thee shall be brass, and the earth that is under thee shall be iron."

"Cursed shalt thou be in the city, and cursed shalt thou be in the field."

"I will make my arrows drunk with blood."

"I will laugh at their calamity."

Did these curses, these threats, come from the heart of love or from the mouth of savagery?

Was Jehovah god or devil?

Why should we place Jehovah above all the gods?

Has man in his ignorance and fear ever imagined a greater monster?

Have the barbarians of any land, in any time, worshipped a more heartless god?

Brahma was a thousand times nobler, and so was Osiris and Zeus and Jupiter. So was the supreme god of the Aztecs, to whom they offered only the perfume of flowers. The worst god of the Hindus, with his necklace of skulls and his bracelets of living snakes, was kind and merciful compared with Jehovah.

Compared with Marcus Aurelius, how small Jehovah seems. Compared with Abraham Lincoln, how cruel, how contemptible, is this god.

VI
JEHOVAH'S ADMINISTRATION

HE created the world, the hosts of heaven, a man and woman—placed them in a garden. Then the serpent deceived them, and they were cast out and made to earn their bread.

Jehovah had been thwarted.

Then he tried again. He went on for about sixteen hundred years trying to civilize the people.

No schools, no churches, no Bible, no tracts—nobody taught to read or write. No Ten Commandments. The people grew worse and worse, until the merciful Jehovah sent the flood and drowned all the people except Noah and his family, eight in all.

Then he started again, and changed their diet. At first Adam and Eve were vegetarians. After the flood Jehovah said: "Every moving thing that liveth shall be meat for you"—snakes and buzzards.

Then he failed again, and at the Tower of Babel he dispersed and scattered the people.

Finding that he could not succeed with all the people, he thought he would try a few, so he selected Abraham and his descendants. Again he failed, and his chosen people were captured by the Egyptians and enslaved for four hundred years.

Then he tried again—rescued them from Pharaoh and started for Palestine.

Then he changed their diet, allowing them to eat only the beasts that parted the hoof and chewed the cud. Again he failed. The people hated him, and preferred the slavery of Egypt to the freedom of Jehovah. So he kept them wandering until nearly all who came from Egypt had died. Then he tried again—took them into Palestine and had them governed by judges.

This, too, was a failure—no schools, no Bible. Then he tried kings, and the kings were mostly idolaters.

Then the chosen people were conquered and carried into captivity by the Babylonians.

Another failure.

Then they returned, and Jehovah tried prophets—howlers and wailers—but the people grew worse and worse. No schools, no sciences, no arts, no commerce. Then Jehovah took upon himself flesh, was born of a woman, and lived among the people that he had been trying to civilize for several thousand years. Then these people, following the law that Jehovah had given them in the wilderness, charged this Jehovah-man—this Christ—with blasphemy; tried, convicted and killed him.

Jehovah had failed again.

Then he deserted the Jews and turned his attention to the rest of the world.

And now the Jews, deserted by Jehovah, persecuted by Christians, are the most prosperous people on the earth. Again has Jehovah failed.

What an administration!

VII
THE NEW TESTAMENT

WHO wrote the New Testament?

Christian scholars admit that they do not know. They admit that, if the four gospels were written by-Matthew, Mark, Luke and John, they must have been written in Hebrew. And yet a Hebrew manuscript of any one of these gospels has never been found. All have been and are in Greek. So, educated theologians admit that the Epistles, James and Jude, were written by persons who had never seen one of the four gospels. In these Epistles— in James and Jude—no reference is made to any of the gospels, nor to any miracle recorded in them.

The first mention that has been found of one of our gospels was made about one hundred and eighty years after the birth of Christ, and the four gospels were first named and quoted from at the beginning of the Third Century, about one hundred and seventy years after the death of Christ.

We now know that there were many other gospels besides our four, some of which have been lost. There were the gospels of Paul, of the Egyptians, of the Hebrews, of Perfection, of Judas, of Thaddeus, of the Infancy, of Thomas, of Mary, of Andrew, of Nicodemus, of Marcion and several others.

So there were the Acts of Pilate, of Andrew, of Mary, of Paul and Thecla and of many others. Another book called the Shepherd of Hermes.

At first not one of all the books was considered as inspired. The Old Testament was regarded as divine; but the books that now constitute the New Testament were regarded as human productions. We now know that we do not know who wrote the four gospels.

The question is, Were the authors of these four gospels inspired?

If they were inspired, then the four gospels must be true. If they are true, they must agree.

The four gospels do not agree.

Matthew, Mark and Luke knew nothing of the Atonement, nothing of salvation by faith. They knew only the gospel of good deeds—of charity. They teach that if we forgive others God will forgive us.

With this the gospel of John does not agree.

In that gospel we are taught that we must believe on the Lord Jesus Christ; that we must be born again; that we must drink the blood and eat the flesh of Christ. In this gospel we find the doctrine of the Atonement and that Christ died for us and suffered in our place.

This gospel is utterly at variance with the other three. If the other three are true, the gospel of John is false. If the gospel of John was written by an inspired man, the writers of the other three were uninspired. From this there is no possible escape. The four cannot be true.

It is evident that there are many interpolations in the four gospels.

For instance, in the 28th chapter of Matthew is an account to the effect that the soldiers at the tomb of Christ were bribed to say that the disciples of Jesus stole away his body while they, the soldiers, slept.

This is clearly an interpolation. It is a break in the narrative.

The 10th verse should be followed by the 16th. The 10th verse is as follows:

"Then Jesus said unto them, 'Be not afraid; go tell my brethren that they go unto Galilee and there shall they see me.'"

The 16th verse:

"Then the eleven disciples went away unto Galilee into a mountain, where Jesus had appointed them."

The story about the soldiers contained in the 11th, 12th, 13th, 14th and 15th verses is an interpolation—an afterthought—long after. The 15th verse demonstrates this.

Fifteenth verse: "So they took the money and did as they were taught. And this saying is commonly reported among the Jews until this day."

Certainly, this account was not in the original gospel, and certainly the 15th verse was not written by a Jew. No Jew could have written this: "And this saying is commonly reported among the Jews until this day."

Mark, John and Luke never heard that the soldiers had been bribed by the priests; or, if they had, did not think it worth while recording. So the accounts of the Ascension of Jesus Christ in Mark and Luke are interpolations. Matthew says nothing about the Ascension.

Certainly there never was a greater miracle, and yet Matthew, who was present—who saw the Lord rise, ascend and disappear—did not think it worth mentioning.

On the other hand, the last words of Christ, according to Matthew, contradict the Ascension: "Lo I am with you always, even unto the end of the world."

John, who was present, if Christ really ascended, says not one word on the subject.

As to the Ascension, the gospels do not agree.

Mark gives the last conversation that Christ had with his disciples, as follows:

"Go ye into all the world and preach the gospel to every creature. He that believeth and is baptised shall be saved; but he that believeth not shall be damned. And these signs shall follow them that believe: In my name shall they cast out devils; they shall speak with new tongues. They shall take up serpents, and if they drink any deadly thing it shall not hurt them; they shall lay hands on the sick and they shall recover. So, then, after the Lord had spoken unto them, he was received up into heaven and sat on the right hand of God."

Is it possible that this description was written by one who witnessed this miracle?

This miracle is described by Luke as follows: "And it came to pass while he blessed them he was parted from them and carried up into heaven."

"Brevity is the soul of wit."

In the Acts we are told that: "When he had spoken, while they beheld, he was taken up, and a cloud received him out of their sight."

Neither Luke, nor Matthew, nor John, nor the writer of the Acts, heard one word of the conversation attributed to Christ by Mark. The fact is that the Ascension of Christ was not claimed by his disciples.

At first Christ was a man—nothing more. Mary was his mother, Joseph his father. The genealogy of his father, Joseph, was given to show that he was of the blood of David.

Then the claim was made that he was the son of God, and that his mother was a virgin, and that she remained a virgin until her death.

Then the claim was made that Christ rose from the dead and ascended bodily to heaven.

It required many years for these absurdities to take possession of the minds of men.

If Christ rose from the dead, why did he not appear to his enemies? Why did he not call on Caiphas, the high priest? Why did he not make another triumphal entry into Jerusalem?

If he really ascended, why did he not do so in public, in the presence of his persecutors? Why should this, the greatest of miracles, be done in secret in a corner?

It was a miracle that could have been seen by a vast multitude — a miracle that could not be simulated — one that would have convinced hundreds of thousands.

After the story of the Resurrection, the Ascension became a necessity. They had to dispose of the body.

So there are many other interpolations in the gospels and epistles.

Again I ask: Is the New Testament true? Does anybody now believe that at the birth of Christ there was a celestial greeting; that a star led the Wise Men of the East; that Herod slew the babes of Bethlehem of two years old and under?

The gospels are filled with accounts of miracles. Were they ever performed?

Matthew gives the particulars of about twenty-two miracles, Mark of about nineteen, Luke of about eighteen and John of about seven.

According to the gospels, Christ healed diseases, cast out devils, rebuked the sea, cured the blind, fed multitudes with five loaves and two fishes, walked on the sea, cursed a fig tree, turned water into wine and raised the dead.

Matthew is the only one that tells about the Star and the Wise Men — the only one that tells about the murder of babes.

John is the only one who says anything about the resurrection of Lazarus, and Luke is the only one giving an account of the raising from the dead the widow of Nain's son.

How is it possible to substantiate these miracles?

The Jews, among whom they were said to have been performed, did not believe them. The diseased, the palsied, the leprous, the blind who were cured, did not become followers of Christ. Those that were raised from the dead were never heard of again.

Does any intelligent man believe in the existence of devils? The writer of three of the gospels certainly did. John says nothing about Christ having cast out devils, but Matthew, Mark and Luke give many instances.

Does any natural man now believe that Christ cast out devils? If his disciples said he did, they were mistaken. If Christ said he did, he was insane or an impostor.

If the accounts of casting out devils are false, then the writers were ignorant or dishonest. If they wrote through ignorance, then they were not inspired. If they wrote what they knew to be false, they were not inspired. If what they wrote is untrue, whether they knew it or not, they were not inspired.

At that time it was believed that palsy, epilepsy, deafness, insanity and many other diseases were caused by devils; that devils took possession of and lived in the bodies of men and women. Christ believed this, taught this belief to others, and pretended to cure diseases by casting devils out of the sick and insane. We know now, if we know anything, that diseases are not caused by the presence of devils. We know, if we know anything, that devils do not reside in the bodies of men.

If Christ said and did what the writers of the three gospels say he said and did, then Christ was mistaken. If he was mistaken, certainly he was not God. And, if he was mistaken, certainly he was not inspired.

Is it a fact that the Devil tried to bribe Christ?

Is it a fact that the Devil carried Christ to the top of the temple and tried to induce him to leap to the ground?

How can these miracles be established?

The principals have written nothing, Christ has written nothing, and the Devil has remained silent.

How can we know that the Devil tried to bribe Christ? Who wrote the account? We do not know. How did the writer get his information? We do not know.

Somebody, some seventeen hundred years ago, said that the Devil tried to bribe God; that the Devil carried God to the top of the temple and tried to induce him to leap to the earth and that God was intellectually too keen for the Devil.

This is all the evidence we have.

Is there anything in the literature of the world more perfectly idiotic?

Intelligent people no longer believe in witches, wizards, spooks and devils, and they are perfectly satisfied that every word in the New Testament about casting out devils is utterly false.

Can we believe that Christ raised the dead?

A widow living in Nain is following the body of her son to the tomb. Christ halts the funeral procession and raises the young man from the dead and gives him back to the arms of his mother.

This young man disappears. He is never heard of again. No one takes the slightest interest in the man who returned from the realm of death. Luke is the only one who tells the story. Maybe Matthew, Mark and John never heard of it, or did not believe it and so failed to record it.

John says that Lazarus was raised from the dead; Matthew, Mark and Luke say nothing about it.

It was more wonderful than the raising of the widow's son. He had not been laid in the tomb for days. He was only on his way to the grave, but Lazarus was actually dead. He had begun to decay.

Lazarus did not excite the least interest. No one asked him about the other world. No one inquired of him about their dead friends.

When he died the second time no one said: "He is not afraid. He has traveled that road twice and knows just where he is going."

We do not believe in the miracles of Mohammed, and yet they are as well attested as this. We have no confidence in the miracles performed by Joseph Smith, and yet the evidence is far greater, far better.

If a man should go about now pretending to raise the dead, pretending to cast out devils, we would regard him as insane. What, then, can we say of Christ? If we wish to save his reputation we are compelled to say that he never pretended to raise the dead; that he never claimed to have cast out devils.

We must take the ground that these ignorant and impossible things were invented by zealous disciples, who sought to deify their leader.

In those ignorant days these falsehoods added to the fame of Christ. But now they put his character in peril and belittle the authors of the gospels.

Can we now believe that water was changed into wine? John tells of this childish miracle, and says that the other disciples were present, yet Matthew, Mark and Luke say nothing about it.

Take the miracle of the man cured by the pool of Bethseda. John says that an angel troubled the waters of the pool of Bethseda, and that whoever got into the pool first after the waters were troubled was healed.

Does anybody now believe that an angel went into the pool and troubled the waters? Does anybody now think that the poor wretch who got in first was healed? Yet the author of the gospel according to John believed and asserted these absurdities. If he was mistaken about that he may have been about all the miracles he records.

John is the only one who tells about this pool of Bethseda. Possibly the other disciples did not believe the story.

How can we account for these pretended miracles?

In the days of the disciples, and for many centuries after, the world was filled with the supernatural. Nearly everything that happened was regarded as miraculous. God was the immediate governor of the world. If the people were good, God sent seed time and harvest; but if they were bad he sent flood and hail, frost and famine. If anything wonderful happened it was exaggerated until it became a miracle.

Of the order of events—of the unbroken and the unbreakable chain of causes and effects—the people had no knowledge and no thought.

A miracle is the badge and brand of fraud. No miracle ever was performed. No intelligent, honest man ever pretended to perform a miracle, and never will.

If Christ had wrought the miracles attributed to him; if he had cured the palsied and insane; if he had given hearing to the deaf, vision to the blind; if he had cleansed the leper with a word, and with a touch had given life and feeling to the withered limb; if he had given pulse and motion, warmth and thought, to cold and breathless clay; if he had conquered death and rescued from the grave its pallid prey—no word would have been uttered, no hand raised, except in praise and honor. In his presence all heads would have been uncovered—all knees upon the ground.

Is it not strange that at the trial of Christ no one was found to say a word in his favor? No man stood forth and said: "I was a leper, and this man cured me with a touch." No woman said: "I am the widow of Nain and this is my son whom this man raised from the dead."

No man said: "I was blind, and this man gave me sight."

All silent.

VIII
THE PHILOSOPHY OF CHRIST

MILLIONS assert that the philosophy of Christ is perfect—that he was the wisest that ever uttered speech.

Let us see:

Resist not evil. If smitten on one cheek turn the other.

Is there any philosophy, any wisdom in this? Christ takes from goodness, from virtue, from the truth, the right of self-defense. Vice becomes the master of the world, and the good become the victims of the infamous.

No man has the right to protect himself, his property, his wife and children. Government becomes impossible, and the world is at the mercy of criminals. Is there any absurdity beyond this?

Love your enemies.

Is this possible? Did any human being ever love his enemies? Did Christ love his, when he denounced them as whited sepulchers, hypocrites and vipers?

We cannot love those who hate us. Hatred in the hearts of others does not breed love in ours. Not to resist evil is absurd; to love your enemies is impossible.

Take no thought for the morrow.

The idea was that God would take care of us as he did of sparrows and lilies. Is there the least sense in that belief?

Does God take care of anybody?

Can we live without taking thought for the morrow? To plow, to sow, to cultivate, to harvest, is to take thought for the morrow. We plan and work for the future, for our children, for the unborn generations to come. Without this forethought there could be no progress, no civilization. The world would go back to the caves and dens of savagery.

If thy right eye offend thee, pluck it out. If thy right hand offend thee, cut it off.

Why? Because it is better that one of our members should perish than that the whole body should be cast into hell.

Is there any wisdom in putting out your eyes or cutting off your hands? Is it possible to extract from these extravagant sayings the smallest grain of common sense?

Swear not at all; neither by Heaven, for it is God's throne; nor by the Earth, for it is his footstool; nor by Jerusalem, for it is his holy city.

Here we find the astronomy and geology of Christ. Heaven is the throne of God, the monarch; the earth is his footstool. A footstool that turns over at the rate of a thousand miles an hour, and sweeps through space at the rate of over a thousand miles a minute!

Where did Christ think heaven was? Why was Jerusalem a holy city? Was it because the inhabitants were ignorant, cruel and superstitious?

If a man sue thee at law and take away your coat, give him your cloak also.

Is there any philosophy, any good sense, in that commandment? Would it not be just as sensible to say: "If a man obtains a judgment against you for one hundred dollars, give him two hundred."

Only the insane could give or follow this advice.

Think not I am come to send peace on earth, I came not to send peace, but a sword. For I am come to set a man at variance against his father, and the daughter against her mother.

If this is true, how much better it would have been had he remained away.

Is it possible that he who said, "Resist not evil," came to bring a sword? That he who said, "Love your enemies," came to destroy the peace of the world?

To set father against son, and daughter against father—what a glorious mission!

He did bring a sword, and the sword was wet for a thousand years with innocent blood. In millions of hearts he sowed the seeds of hatred and revenge. He divided nations and families, put out the light of reason, and petrified the hearts of men.

And every one that hath forsaken houses, or brethren, or sisters, or father, or mother, or wife, or children, or lands, for my name's sake, shall receive an hundredfold, and shall inherit everlasting life.

According to the writer of Matthew, Christ, the compassionate, the merciful, uttered these terrible words. Is it possible that Christ offered the bribe of eternal joy to those who would desert their fathers, their mothers, their wives and children? Are we to win the happiness of heaven by deserting the ones we love? Is a home to be ruined here for the sake of a mansion there?

And yet it is said that Christ is an example for all the world. Did he desert his father and mother? He said, speaking to his mother: "Woman, what have I to do with thee?"

The Pharisees said unto Christ: "Is it lawful to pay tribute unto Caesar?"

Christ said: "Show me the tribute money." They brought him a penny. And he saith unto them: "Whose is the image and the superscription?" They said: "Caesar's." And Christ said: "Render unto Caesar the things that are Caesar's."

Did Christ think that the money belonged to Caesar because his image and superscription were stamped upon it? Did the penny belong to Caesar or to the man who had earned it? Had Caesar the right to demand it because it was adorned with his image?

Does it appear from this conversation that Christ understood the real nature and use of money?

Can we now say that Christ was the greatest of philosophers?

IX
IS CHRIST OUR EXAMPLE?

HE never said a word in favor of education. He never even hinted at the existence of any science. He never uttered a word in favor of industry, economy or of any effort to better our condition in this world. He was the enemy of the successful, of the wealthy. Dives was sent to hell, not because he was bad, but because he was rich. Lazarus went to heaven, not because he was good, but because he was poor.

Christ cared nothing for painting, for sculpture, for music—nothing for any art. He said nothing about the duties of nation to nation, of king to subject; nothing about the rights of man; nothing about intellectual liberty or the freedom of speech. He said nothing about the sacredness of home; not one word for the fireside; not a word in favor of marriage, in honor of maternity.

He never married. He wandered homeless from place to place with a few disciples. None of them seem to have been engaged in any useful business, and they seem to have lived on alms.

All human ties were held in contempt; this world was sacrificed for the next; all human effort was discouraged. God would support and protect.

At last, in the dusk of death, Christ, finding that he was mistaken, cried out: "My God! My God! Why hast thou forsaken me?"

We have found that man must depend on himself. He must clear the land; he must build the home; he must plow and plant; he must invent; he must work with hand and brain; he must overcome the difficulties and obstructions; he must conquer and enslave the forces of nature to the end that they may do the work of the world.

X

WHY SHOULD WE PLACE CHRIST AT THE TOP AND SUMMIT OF THE HUMAN RACE?

WAS he kinder, more forgiving, more self-sacrificing than Buddha? Was he wiser, did he meet death with more perfect calmness, than Socrates? Was he more patient, more charitable, than Epictetus? Was he a greater philosopher, a deeper thinker, than Epicurus? In what respect was he the superior of Zoroaster? Was he gentler than Laotse, more universal than Confucius? Were his ideas of human rights and duties superior to those of Zeno? Did he express grander truths than Cicero? Was his mind subtler than Spinoza's? Was his brain equal to Kepler's or Newton's? Was he grander in death—a sublimer martyr than Bruno? Was he in intelligence, in the force and beauty of expression, in breadth and scope of thought, in wealth of illustration, in aptness of comparison, in knowledge of the human brain and heart, of all passions, hopes and fears, the equal of Shakespeare, the greatest of the human race?

If Christ was in fact God, he knew all the future.

Before him like a panorama moved the history yet to be. He knew how his words would be interpreted. He knew what crimes, what horrors, what infamies, would be committed in his name. He knew that the hungry flames of persecution would climb around the limbs of countless martyrs. He knew that thousands and thousands of brave men and women would languish in dungeons in darkness, filled with pain. He knew that his church would invent and use instruments of torture; that his followers would appeal to whip and fagot, to chain and rack. He saw the horizon of the future lurid with the flames of the auto-da-fê. He knew what creeds would spring like poisonous fungi from every text. He saw the ignorant sects waging war against each other. He saw thousands of men, under the orders of priests, building prisons for their fellow-men. He saw thousands of scaffolds dripping with the best and bravest blood. He saw his followers using the instruments of pain. He heard the groans—saw the faces white with agony. He heard the shrieks and sobs and cries of all the moaning, martyred multitudes. He knew that commentaries would be written on his words with swords, to be read by the light of fagots. He knew that the Inquisition would be born of the teachings attributed to him.

He saw the interpolations and falsehoods that hypocrisy would write and tell. He saw all wars that would be waged, and he knew that above these fields of death, these dungeons, these rackings, these burnings, these executions, for a thousand years would float the dripping banner of the cross.

He knew that hypocrisy would be robed and crowned — that cruelty and credulity would rule the world; knew that liberty would perish from the earth; knew that popes and kings in his name would enslave the souls and bodies of men; knew that they would persecute and destroy the discoverers, thinkers and inventors; knew that his church would extinguish reason's holy light and leave the world without a star.

He saw his disciples extinguishing the eyes of men, flaying them alive, cutting out their tongues, searching for all the nerves of pain.

He knew that in his name his followers would trade in human flesh; that cradles would be robbed and women's breasts unbabed for gold.

And yet he died with voiceless lips.

Why did he fail to speak? Why did he not tell his disciples, and through them the world: "You shall not burn, imprison and torture in my name. You shall not persecute your fellow-men."

Why did he not plainly say: "I am the Son of God," or, "I am God?" Why did he not explain the Trinity? Why did he not tell the mode of baptism that was pleasing to him? Why did he not write a creed? Why did he not break the chains of slaves? Why did he not say that the Old Testament was or was not the inspired word of God? Why did he not write the New Testament himself? Why did he leave his words to ignorance, hypocrisy and chance? Why did he not say something positive, definite and satisfactory about another world? Why did he not turn the tear-stained hope of heaven into the glad knowledge of another life? Why did he not tell us something of the rights of man, of the liberty of hand and brain?

Why did he go dumbly to his death, leaving the world to misery and to doubt?

I will tell you why. He was a man, and did not know.

XI
INSPIRATION

NOT before about the Third Century was it claimed or believed that the books composing the New Testament were inspired.

It will be remembered that there were a great number of books, of Gospels, Epistles and Acts, and that from these the "inspired" ones were selected by "uninspired" men.

Between the "Fathers" there were great differences of opinion as to which books were inspired; much discussion and plenty of hatred. Many of the books now deemed spurious were by many of the "Fathers" regarded as divine, and some now regarded as inspired were believed to be spurious. Many of the early Christians and some of the "Fathers" repudiated the gospel of John, the Epistle to the Hebrews, Jude, James, Peter, and the Revelation of St. John. On the other hand, many of them regarded the Gospel of the Hebrews, of the Egyptians, the Preaching of Peter, the Shepherd of Hermas, the Epistle of Barnabus, the Pastor of Hermas, the Revelation of Peter, the Revelation of Paul, the Epistle of Clement, the Gospel of Nicodemus, inspired books, equal to the very best.

From all these books, and many others, the Christians selected the inspired ones.

The men who did the selecting were ignorant and superstitious. They were firm believers in the miraculous. They thought that diseases had been cured by the aprons and handkerchiefs of the apostles, by the bones of the dead. They believed in the fable of the Phoenix, and that the hyenas changed their sex every year.

Were the men who through many centuries made the selections inspired? Were they—ignorant, credulous, stupid and malicious—as well qualified to judge of "inspiration" as the students of our time? How are we bound by their opinion? Have we not the right to judge for ourselves?

Erasmus, one of the leaders of the Reformation, declared that the Epistle to the Hebrews was not written by Paul, and he denied the inspiration of Second and Third John, and also of Revelation. Luther was of the same opinion. He declared James to be an epistle of straw, and denied the inspiration of Revelations. Zwinglius rejected the book of Revelation, and even Calvin denied that Paul was the author of Hebrews.

The truth is that the Protestants did not agree as to what books are inspired until 1647, by the Assembly of Westminster.

To prove that a book is inspired you must prove the existence of God. You must also prove that this God thinks, acts, has objects, ends and aims. This is somewhat difficult.

It is impossible to conceive of an infinite being. Having no conception of an infinite being, it is impossible to tell whether all the facts we know tend to prove or disprove the existence of such a being.

God is a guess. If the existence of God is admitted, how are we to prove that he inspired the writers of the books of the Bible?

How can one man establish the inspiration of another? How can an inspired man prove that he is inspired? How can he know himself that he is inspired? There is no way to prove the fact of inspiration. The only evidence is the word of some man who could by no possibility know anything on the subject.

What is inspiration? Did God use men as instruments? Did he cause them to write his thoughts? Did he take possession of their minds and destroy their wills?

Were these writers only partly controlled, so that their mistakes, their ignorance and their prejudices were mingled with the wisdom of God?

How are we to separate the mistakes of man from the thoughts of God? Can we do this without being inspired ourselves? If the original writers were inspired, then the translators should have been, and so should be the men who tell us what the Bible means.

How is it possible for a human being to know that he is inspired by an infinite being? But of one thing we may be certain: An inspired book should certainly excel all the books produced by uninspired men. It should, above all, be true, filled with wisdom, blossoming in beauty—perfect.

Ministers wonder how I can be wicked enough to attack the Bible.

I will tell them:

This book, the Bible, has persecuted, even unto death, the wisest and the best. This book stayed and stopped the onward movement of the human race. This book poisoned the fountains of learning and misdirected the energies of man.

This book is the enemy of freedom, the support of slavery. This book sowed the seeds of hatred in families and nations, fed the flames of war, and impoverished the world. This book is the breastwork of kings and tyrants—the enslaver of women and children. This book has corrupted parliaments and courts. This book has made colleges and universities the teachers of error and the haters of science. This book has filled Christendom with hateful, cruel, ignorant and warring sects. This book taught men to kill their fellows for religion's sake. This book founded the inquisition, invented the instruments of torture, built the dungeons in which the good and loving languished, forged the chains that rusted in their flesh, erected the scaffolds whereon they died. This book piled fagots about the feet of the just. This book drove reason from the minds of millions and filled the asylums with the insane.

This book has caused fathers and mothers to shed the blood of their babes. This book was the auction block on which the slave-mother stood when she was sold from her child. This book filled the sails of the slave-trader and made merchandise of human flesh. This book lighted the fires that burned "witches" and "wizards." This book filled the darkness with ghouls and ghosts, and the bodies of men and women with devils. This book polluted the souls of men with the infamous dogma of eternal pain. This book made credulity the greatest of virtues, and investigation the greatest of crimes. This book filled nations with hermits, monks and nuns—with the pious and the useless. This book placed the ignorant and unclean saint above the philosopher and philanthropist. This book taught man to despise the joys of this life, that he might be happy in another—to waste this world for the sake of the next.

I attack this book because it is the enemy of human liberty—the greatest obstruction across the highway of human progress.

Let me ask the ministers one question: How can you be wicked enough to defend this book?

XII
THE REAL BIBLE

FOR thousands of years men have been writing the real Bible, and it is being written from day to day, and it will never be finished while man has life. All the facts that we know, all the truly recorded events, all the discoveries and inventions, all the wonderful machines whose wheels and levers seem to think, all the poems, crystals from the brain, flowers from the heart, all the songs of love and joy, of smiles and tears, the great dramas of Imagination's world, the wondrous paintings, miracles of form and color, of light and shade, the marvellous marbles that seem to live and breathe, the secrets told by rock and star, by dust and flower, by rain and snow, by frost and flame, by winding stream and desert sand, by mountain range and billowed sea.

All the wisdom that lengthens and ennobles life—all that avoids or cures disease, or conquers pain—all just and perfect laws and rules that guide and shape our lives, all thoughts that feed the flames of love, the music that transfigures, enraptures and enthralls, the victories of heart and brain, the miracles that hands have wrought, the deft and cunning hands of those who worked for wife and child, the histories of noble deeds, of brave and useful men, of faithful loving wives, of quenchless mother-love, of conflicts for the right, of sufferings for the truth, of all the best that all the men and women of the world have said, and thought and done through all the years.

These treasures of the heart and brain—these are the Sacred Scriptures of the human race.